Do We Ever Stay?

Do We Ever Stay?

Poems by

Susan Hunter

© 2026 Susan Hunter. All rights reserved.
This material may not be reproduced in any form, published,
reprinted, recorded, performed, broadcast,
rewritten or redistributed without
the explicit permission of Susan Hunter.
All such actions are strictly prohibited by law.

Cover design by Shay Culligan
Cover image by Eugene Chystiakov on Unsplash
Author photo by Arnie Weiss

ISBN: 978-1-63980-962-2
Library of Congress Control Number: 2026931376

Kelsay Books
502 South 1040 East, A-119
American Fork, Utah 84003
Kelsaybooks.com

*For my family—
past, present and future*

Acknowledgments

To friends and family members for offering continued support, encouragement and appreciation.

To the late poet and professor, Robert Pack, for inspiring me many years ago in his poetry classes and in recent years as our paths crossed again, helping guide me along my poetic journey.

To Stephan Delbos, former poet laureate of Plymouth, Massachusetts, for giving me opportunities to share my poetry and for suggesting ways to organize my book.

To Miriam O'Neal, Plymouth's current poet laureate, for providing events and creative spaces for me and other poets to share our work.

Many thanks to the editors of the publications where these poems, or earlier versions of them, have appeared:

The 2024 One Page Poetry Anthology: "Boulanger's 'D'un Vieux Jardin'"
American Literary Review Awards, finalist: "Bread-Makers"
The Chaffin Journal: "On Viewing Childe Hassam," "The Girls' Rooms"
Illya's Honey: "Gone"
On the Seawall: "Christmas Songs"
Poem: "Leaving"
Saranac Review: "Father"
Southern Humanities Review: "Door"

Some of the poems in this collection also appeared in the chapbook *Unfinished Spaces,* published by Finishing Line Press.

Contents

1. Do We Ever Stay?

Christmas Songs	15
The Kitchen	17
Door	19
To You, I Bequeath . . .	20
First Love	22
The Girls' Rooms	23
Unfinished Spaces	24
End of Story During a Pandemic	25
Barrens	27
Grandson	29
To My Granddaughter	30
Astronomy	32
Leaving	34
Thankful	35
Trees	36
In the Woods	38
At the Birdfeeder	40
Lullaby	42
Elsbeth	43
Bread-Makers	44

2. We Say Goodbye

Nantucket	49
Gone	50
Father	51
Dreams of My Father	52
January	54

Susannah	55
Jennie	56
Memorial	58
Spending Time	60
Boulanger's "D'un Vieux Jardin (of an old garden)"	62
Emily Dickinson	63
On Viewing Childe Hassam	64
Artist's Studio	66
Photograph on a Foggy Winter Afternoon	68
Deer	69

3. A World of Sunrise

These Four o'Clock Days	73
Window Witch	74
Wooster Square, 2020	76
Cape Cod Bay	78
Beach	79
Maine Sunrise	80
Marigot	82
Caribbean Rising	84
Dominoes	86
Monument Valley	87
Tucson	88
Seville Sunday	89
Massachusetts	90
What We Have, in Plymouth	92
Boston	94

1. Do We Ever Stay?

Christmas Songs

I listen to those Christmas songs
playing in the doctor's office
in the stale days before the new year breaks.
Let's have done with frenzy, ribbons and the miles
between then and now, between them and now.

The year sags, the hammock of winter
holds aching bones, curved spine.
I can think only of champagne catching the tree lights
through the Millennium goblets I bought in Ireland
it seems a thousand years ago.

The sparkling wine rushes the forehead
to welcome the new days.
Children's voices move away,
piano keys grow silent, suitcases are packed full.

Do we ever stay?
The new daylight goes unnoticed.
The swimming pool lies under its moldy, canvas top.
Faded poinsettia leaves, brown over white,
struggle into a February that sees
roses bend their necked stems in silent death throes.

Did I just hear another Christmas carol
pressed like a dead petal within a television jingle?
Why don't we let it go?
A little girl, a stranger,
now strikes the keys of my family piano
that I had to leave behind.

I saw the piano move down an angled plank
and up another into the van,
Was my mother watching also?
The years of Christmas carols
trailed behind, as the truck
moved down the summer road.

The Kitchen

It was a different room,
when I came back,
smell of mold, the broken dishwasher
still unemptied after 30 years.
I didn't belong there, and it didn't
belong to me.

What I came back to was a new space,
new and ancient, so old
it seemed it had never
felt Neuman's ghost
standing in front of the refrigerator
on his funeral day.

The kitchen so old I had never gazed out the window
at an early October snowstorm,
watched my daughter hold a cat by its haunches,
saw the summer kale itching to be picked.

The room didn't welcome me.
Soon, dishtowels draped chair backs,
the toilet broke,
and at the tag sale in the driveway,
I found the plaster cast of the hand
I had made in kindergarten.
Heartline severed, one flayed branch
heading off to the north, one to the south,

never meant to catch love
in its palm.

Broken heartline always heading away to strange rooms.
Me, the spirit, packing up, unwelcomed.

Door

Door I'd come in and out
and in and out with lilacs in my hands,
angry over her, over him, over her and over him.

Door I came through after ice and snow.
Door she bolted to keep us out.
Door I ran out of to do what I loved.

Door my daughter slammed.
Door the ghost came through
with house-warming embrace.

Door closed after I had left.
Sound of shutting,
of breaking heart apart.

To You, I Bequeath . . .

I'll take them all with me in sacks.
Fantasies, bad dreams,
cars heading nowhere,
lost grocery bags,
lost grandchildren,
those who wouldn't listen,
illnesses that won't quit.

Or, I'll leave them all behind,
a momentous irresponsibility.
I'm done with all this,
and you can do what you want with it.

It will be stacked on a bookshelf
next to my moldy diplomas,
picture of my great grandmother,
poster I bought when I danced
in a sheared beaver coat.

All the stuff.
For you to decide.

I'm taking my life with me,
stronger than ever,
still burning with whatever
keeps my imperfect heart going.

I'm leaving a Korean mother-of-pearl box,
a bookmark, a gold clock.

Just don't throw it all away.
I've written something
over the years, for you.

First Love

You don't deserve a poem,
but your undeserving
still drags my thoughts
through soiled waters.

Not like fish-full rivers
in a cold New England spring,
but like that un-running brook
that pools, clotted,
under the bridge.

How strong a magnet's grip
you had on my untouched, green-eyed girl-ness!
I thought all skipped to school
on the chimes of a seminary bell.

You stretched distance from your lakes
to my ocean so tautly I feared dying
from poisoned mosquitoes
before I saw you again.

Hop-scotching across puzzled floors,
foot plunging through missing pieces,
ankle twisted,
I fell straight to earth.
awakened by chapel bells.

It was you I died from.

The Girls' Rooms

They're empty of girls now,
and what stays are the smiles
of those you knew
pasted in collages stuck to the walls.

Pets' ashes lie in small boxes,
and stuffed animals bask in sunlight
that pours through lacy curtains not heavy
enough to keep out the cold.

The clothes that didn't go with them hang
In all the dusty rooms that dot the seacoast
where guests sleep, glancing at
biology papers and bunches of fake flowers.

A guitar sits in one corner; a flute is smothered in a bureau drawer.
You crank open the window, let in fresh air,
and close the door.
In the corner, a doll sits on a chair
with tears in her eyes.

Unfinished Spaces

You return often to that house,
walking through the front door,
down the large hall clouded with your father's pipe smoke.
As you head up the stairs,
the mouse circles your mother's feet again.
She laughs as you play the piano in the living room
and chase notes as they run away.

In your grandparents' house,
You spill the jewelry box onto the bedcovers,
while the dancing ballerina does a pirouette
to a hurdy-gurdy sound.

The room where you found your life again
was stripped bare that last night.
You tried to put it back together
forcing stubborn puzzle pieces into a headache.

One day, you'll remember it as it was
on sunny mornings, your young daughter close by,
the woodpecker tapping on the wall,
the white birch scraping its branches across the wood.

End of Story During a Pandemic

The endings are not on the page.
They tell of the last conversation, kindnesses,
gin and tonics in a cabin,
Casablanca on a rainy Cambridge night.

I've searched for my great grandfather
who may have died on a ship
or may have married someone else.
May have been a cleric with a choke collar
cradling his handsome face.
May have loved my great grandmother Jane
and taken all her money.

He was baptized in a small white church
 in County Donegal
and married Jane in Glasgow.
He may have fallen ill in Kansas, but
no one knows his ending.
Few words were spoken of this man
who was born the eldest child
during the first year of the Irish famine.

There were whisperings of too much to drink,
of walking with Jane on Inch Island where
small waves lapped around their ankles
as they ran across a sea of mussel shells.
Sunlight sparkled on the water
before reaching its resting place
on the opposite shore.

How's that for an ending?
How else do you say it ended,
if not with a broken heart?

Sun, how many times will you rise
before this is over?
You top the neighbor's house,
as she walks her dogs gingerly in frosty grass.
She holds the leashes like flounces
of a ball gown.

The endings are not on the page.
Someone will tell the story
when the pages have turned for the last time.
It was a time of illness, they'll say,
that went on and on.
There was a sun-filled room,
and we walked and walked in the woods,
on a journey that never ends.

Barrens

Heat of my childhood I had forgotten
as I stepped out of the car
at the bottom of the state.

Shimmering wetland inlets,
salt-filled air.
The forbidden barren pines'
unfulfilled promise of
canoeing down green rivers,
eyes spying around stunted tree trunks.

It's said the Hessians,
those fighting for the wrong side,
those fleeing everything,
fled to this flat, humid area.
No sight of the ocean,
just green and murky rivers.

Soon a snaky road was built
through it, a gas station or two.
My aunt's car, fresh from Philadelphia,
was bumped from the rear by
those descendants of the pines.

My grandparents drove over that road.
We met them there every summer
own the way to the coast
at a diner filled with the aroma of bacon.

I made the rest of my way
with them, in their car, my grandfather
often crossing that line in the road.

For me, it was a cocoon,
as I rode seatbelt-less
into a summer of large waves,
sunlight, and the promise of forever
that ended in September when
we made our way back home
through those dark woods.

My grandparents have long since gone,
the old road replaced with an expressway
But the pines stay, pushing at
the edges of the peopled world,
not welcoming, but
ushering me once again through the fronds
in my older age.
Wetness drips from their leaves.

Heat of my childhood I had forgotten
as I step from the car,
breathing in the hot moisture,
meeting *my* grandchildren
on the way to the coast.

Grandson

Holding you there on my lap,
in the rocking chair,
in your room that was your room
before you were born,
I want to remember the moment
your eyes turned to the crib
where you usually lie.

Did you see them smiling there,
the ones I can't see anymore,
the ones I never knew?
Or did you begin waking up to
where you are,
where you were
and where you'll be?

I remember myself in adolescent fury
and my grandmother saying,
"You were such a sweet little girl!"

Will I say that also to you?
That you were a sweet little boy
and that I remember
the moment I held you on my lap
in the rocking chair,
in the room that was yours
before you were born?

To My Granddaughter

Shame on me
for not remembering
every minute your smile,
your laugh,
a milk moustache,
somersault on the yoga mat,
dancing to Adele.

You begin to talk to me
heart to heart.
I wish I could give advice,
but it's all yours.

You are the athlete,
running as I hoped you would,
all the way down the field,
soccer ball into the net.

Your small body follows the ball,
hidden among a circle of bigger girls.
And then you and the ball
emerge from the huddle, and
you steer that soccer ball to its goal.

Growing up has
just a few stumbles,
aiming the ball into
smaller and small nets.

Your dog Tedy licks your face.

And there will be more dogs,
and friends
and fishing boats,
sunlight on the harbor.

I can't tell you where you'll go,
or where I'll go,
or when.

On your fifth birthday,
You undid your clothes and ran outside.
you didn't tell us why.

We'll catch the butterfly
that escaped, I promise you.
See its purple edges,
bright yellow ovals,
filled with blue.
We'll find a refuge.

The butterflies rise to
the top of a sunlit tented space,
safe until they head off toward
summer sunshine.

Astronomy

Red maple trees in fall,
morning sunlight on the porch
and Haydn's arias.

The woman scientist said
we should thank our lucky stars
to have lived at this time
of rushing mass propelled by
the big bang.

Our moon, faithful disc,
keeps us both tethered
and sane,
and a child I know asks
"Is heaven far away?"

Look out through the night,
past the sunset striped by heat.
Hold onto my hand
as we spend one last day on the beach,
waves going out, coming in,
out and in.

You throw stones into the water,
and off the cliff, searching for a fin
past the salt-and-pepper sand.

I peer at Comet Neowise
whose filmy fish tail
squirms through Ursa Major.

Keep my universe close . . .
sun brightening wildflowers,
a seashell in a small hand,
mist painting hills on the river's far bank.

Leaving

The last times go unrecognized.
How dense, fog-draped we are
at candlelit dinner tables,
on porches with rocking chairs
facing the ocean.
A tennis ball streaks over the net,
and a thousand nights pass unnoticed
before you all leave.

No warning when you go,
that it will be forever,
that there will be silence
as deep and dark as unmoving pines.

How do we not fret as you leave us
to shelter our children?
We have no preparation for what is
etched into shadows, the sagging skin,
hieroglyphics on the tomb.

Thankful

If memory is fickle,
I didn't travel to a small, zinc-smelting town
elbowed to the side of Blue Mountain
on Thanksgiving.
My aunt, denizen of her Pennsylvania hamlet,
arose at 5 a.m. to start cooking.
Turkey melting off its large bones, chestnut stuffing,
potato stuffing, green beans and cranberries,
shoo fly pie and cupcakes, corn and relish salad.

Later, Queenie would stop by
and draw portraits of my brother and me,
her gnarled hands gripping the pencil.
She and her car, my aunt later said,
were hit on the tracks by the 5:13 train
leaving Chicago.

Her portraits of little kids,
barrette in hair, bow tie, were stuffed
in a basement box on subterranean journeys
from one damp New England house to another.

If memory is fickle—or made up—
Pilgrim children dressed in top hats and buckles
didn't sit at a long table with Indians
enjoying turkey and cranberries.
The feast lasted three days, they say, and all sat
on the ground near the large bay,
thankful for those still alive,
before their grandchildren headed west.

Trees

When I was a child,
in my grandparents' yard,
I'd embrace a large tree trunk
and feel a tug at my hand
from the other side.

When I was older,
three unborn babies
held anger so high
it towered over the trees
in my front yard.

As I raked leaves,
knelt to pull up weeds,
I heard "Mom!" in clear pitch,
a child's voice in the trees.

"I heard you before you were born,"
I'd tell my daughter,
and we ran hand in hand
around those trees,
her small boots shaking the ground.

Were the tree fairies, garden gnomes
playing a cosmic, comic game of hide and seek?
What do they know of hope, grief, patience and love?

The child I finally bore
cares for children of her own,
and they look up through the trees,
as a hawk scatters a flock of crows,
while leaves spiral, coiled from the northern sky.

In the Woods

I imagine that I hadn't heard.

I would have gone on walking,
kicking moldy leaves,
my sneakers wet
in the summer rivulets.

I would have watched our dog
plunge down the bank
into the creek and shake himself dry.

I would not have heard
a cell phone ringing,
just up from my pocket.

It was about my heart.
"No possible medication, only surgery."
I wondered, could I travel to Maine
to see the sunset again, the boat's wake
in the moonlight?
"I'm not God," the doctor said.

As a child, I'd cover my ears with my small hands,
not to hear the cricket caught in my bedroom closet.

But now, as I jumped a fissure
between what lay before and what lay ahead
I saw the Dog had rejoined us.
Maybe not God, but fateful reversal.
I saw the nuthatch soar into the sun.

At the Birdfeeder

I think it's the birds I will miss most.
When you think of their feathers,
bright yellow against black, white against gray.

I hear their songs when early spring
crawls across the soil.
So hopeful, those three notes,
the invisible bird
hides in unblossomed branches.

I recall the robin's song that is my childhood,
the upright wet grass balancing
a cracked bird's egg.

My daughter thinks a cardinal is my mother,
and I could believe them ethereal.
But with us, they wait and wait for warm weather,
wait for sunlight to warm the sand.

Today, when we walk the beach,
a gull moves head-on toward us,
daring and cock-sure.
Those sandpipers, as if tied together,
shift as one body through the mirror wave.

I think about the birds
springing off the ground
and flying over everything we live in—

the almost perfect harbor and the thread
of a road tied taut to a knob of land
in the middle of the bay.

I thought about praying to a cardinal
when I was sick,
cynical eyes open,
and feeling better soon.
I gave my mother's cardinal painting
to my daughter.
It watches over her house,
waiting for spring.

Lullaby

The trolley car driver, my great-grandfather,
was newly arrived from Germany,
seven children in tow.
Grief drove him through the streets, out of his head.

So I was told over the years,
when they spoke of my great-grandmother's death.
It was a drunk doctor, they said,
and she died in childbirth.
Baby Lydia lived another half year.

My grandmother was two years old,
and her mother and sister were dead.
And there were stories she told me
about a mourning dove,
fingernail marks inside coffin lids,
a small girl wandering in the woods
as an owl hooted
and flushed a roadside ghost.

As my grandmother grew,
her father made beautiful mandolins for her to sing to.
Over the years, there was left a pocket of air
for a song.
Small fingers plucked the strings,
rooting out demons.
Small voices soared above piano keys.

My grandmother sang warbling measures
as she grew old.
It was music to send her away again,
as Lydia and her mother
rocked to a pale, silent lullaby.

Elsbeth

I was going to talk about my
seventh great-grandmother Elsbeth,
who survived the Swiss Plague in 1611
at the age of one.
Her village, Winterthur, Switzerland,
lost half its townsfolk
in one September week.

Today, while I sit in lockdown
in front of a computer,
it's too easy to imagine Elsbeth's father and grandparents
struggling for breath inside a pitched roof house.

It may have taken years for *that* plague to cross the Alps
and strike the village of Winterthur.
Mountains postponed the disease,
and it could have been just one traveler
hiking with a wooden stick to carry the sickness in.

There's a statue in Vienna celebrating the end of the plague.
Among the stone carvings, a withered woman, hair like snakes,
cowers beside a figure of faith, cross in hand,
gold shining out under a noon-day sun.

In Switzerland in 1611, Elsbeth lived.
She went on to marry Titus Fehr.
Fehr means "ferryman,"
and there were rivers to cross, a shore coming closer.

I was going to talk about Elsbeth,
my seventh great-grandmother,
who survived the Swiss Plague
and thank her for living.

Bread-Makers

They're still emerging from the earth,
these ancestors with my DNA.
Some stones stand tall with "mother"
etched on them, meaning she
labored to bear 13 babies,
and lose two or three.

The grief was no less for each,
but squeezed between rounds of
bread-making, clothes-washing,
metal pot-repairing, vegetable-planting.

No record of these women
in censuses naming them
as household numbers
amongst head of cattle.

I baked bread once on a day of a snowstorm
and felt the whirr of the women,
the bread-makers coaxing me on,
giggling over the oven in the wall
so like the man-sized fireplace
where they flipped the loaves over,
early morning by early morning.

They left the earth,
and the bread burned over the fire
tended by daughters
who kneaded yeasty, tear-salt lumps,
a stone in stomach's pit.

I grieve for the women,
their graves marked dark with
the span of their lives,
their work, the loaves
lost to the grassy Pennsylvania hills.

2. We Say Goodbye

Nantucket

is the place
I went with you.
I'm a girl with brown hair pulled back,
lying in a field of daisies, holding one.

I was smiling at you who just said
 "I wouldn't care if I never saw your mother again."

On the bicycle, I looked back
at your large, pale face.
Not many smiles.
I didn't bring them out.
And on the ferry, you looked at a child rubbing its eyes.
"The baby is tired," you said.

I loved you.
But too many jagged edges
of the very young
didn't fit together,
unthought-out words,
casual in their catastrophe.

Still, it was a perfect island,
shimmering harbor, meadows of grass.
I remember the foghorn
moaning out into the night ocean
as a metronome clocking all the sadness of shipwrecks,
of wives on widows' walks,
of those lost, who never came back.

Gone

In my dream, ticking like a metronome,
I climb the hill to your stone
that's straight and new, like a soldier with
no more stories to tell.
Rain pelts the tooth picked rise and marsh,
and I bring a yellow rose.

Someday, when they get around to it,
they'll inscribe your name
on the roster of spirits
that rise and fall on this hillside.

Someday, a pony-tailed girl
will work on a grave rubbing
and hang it on her wall.

I think how you guided me around your city
before we shared the wine,
and you spoke fluent Spanish to the waiter.
In my dream, you and I sit at either end
of a long, candlelit table.
If memory serves me, you handed me a flower
on a dusky summer evening.

Now, I must hurry away.
The clouds fill and spit
on the cold lake water.
One sweep over the stone,
and I'm gone to find my own slumber.

Father

Outside, through the window,
the frozen pond
is blistering in the January sun.

Here, in the room where my father dies,
the curtains are drawn dark
to shield the world from a life
that has been reduced to a series of gasps.

Amid breathlessness,
the ancient civilizations he studied
don't amount to a hill of beans.

As I glance above his head,
mourning the loss of conversation,
laughter and sweet pipe smoke,

a halo spreads from wall to wall.
Blocks of light, build to a miraculous
shining thing his eyes can't see.

The vision fades too quickly to call witness,
leaving a razor-thin thread of hope
to see him looking once more at me
from the empty holy corner.

Dreams of My Father

In my dream, the summer I went to Korea,
my father was lost,
less than Buddha,
the bronzed god
smiling, fingers in yoga mudra
embracing all,
from the lowest,
who dodged through the narrow street,
clutching a greasy mandu,
to the highest temple monk
who felt the mountain breeze waft through
the wet, heat-charged air.
In child's pose,
knees aching,
the monk bowed toward the giant, smiling statue.

In my dream, my father and I
went to church together.
The minister smiled.
And then, underground, I lost my father
who was dressed in the suit and tie he wore to
Korea that long ago summer.

He took a plane with
propellers grinding.
and greeted people sick of war.
They smiled, and gave him
the keys to open Seoul.

I was young then, just getting by,
hoping he would come home.

"How did you circle the earth alone?"
I should have asked.
Instead, I traveled to that land 50 years later,
and dreamed
that he was lost.
I needed to strike the gong stone
that rang out in the forest.
"My father is gone!"

When he reappeared,

he was a round Buddha-likeness,
sad, like a boy who searched
for the gifts he lost in the temple,
Sad, like the man who misplaced
the mother of pearl he would have given
to the daughter he left behind.

January

Today would have been my mother's 103rd birthday.
The wind blows the tops of the bare trees
as a nor'easter holds course to this hollow.

The sound of the wind
starts high in the woods
and works louder low.

In another season, another place,
late afternoon sunlight moves
up the trees, gathering at the leafy tops
before dispelling a summer day.

Mother, you hear nothing high or low here,
held still in a birthday month,
candle-less, wicks blown to wax.

On a far-away summer day,
Your granddaughter and her friends
play birthday games before
the storm hits.

Safe inside, we watch as
the trees bend lower and lower
before the wind leaves,
straightening the trunks,
scattering memories in the soaked grass.

Susannah

When you learn that someone has gone
who held beauty until her last day,
you remember you were too late
to send her a poem.
But you'll remember her words:
"Rise above it!"

She has left her sunset-filled living room,
ceiling lifted far above the Golden Gate Bridge.
The tsunami she spoke of never struck her house.
The sun-filled living room wasn't crumbled by a quaking wall.

Susannah showed us Muir Woods,
patterned sunlight on the forest floor,
dusty California roads,
the Pacific carving out Point Reyes.

Oh how we've lost!

We look up unable
to catch the sun
through Redwood leaves.
But we can follow its silver trail over the water
from her house to the hills.

Jennie

"You were my best friend," she said,
as she embraced my brother and me.
"You two look so healthy," she said,
from one whose health left her with steely dreams
as the "sneaky" cancer looped from brain,
erasing threads of routine,
and crept down the spine, numbing the legs.

She moved one foot, munched on candy,
worrying about days ahead
and dreaming of driving to Montana.

"I'm thinking of all the things that I can do
without having to walk," she said.
And yes, the sky, the prairie dog houses, super moon,
and the time, dressed in a gingham bonnet,
she drove across the whole damn country.

"I'm going to send an email tomorrow to everyone," she said,

I think of three sisters around a dinner table,
the old dog pacing by Lake Memphremagog.

Soon Jennie will greet her mother
who's riding a horse
through a Jersey spring,
and her father,
smoking that last cigarette
as he looks up from Rimbaud's verse
to catch her eye.

Memorial

It was raining as they lowered you
into a perfect square
in Maryland.

Rows and rows of soaked stones
I saw, like the stripes of faded red and white,
framing your father's Medal of Honor.

At the gravesite, friends tossed long stemmed roses
and told stories of a boy,
life's sadness weaving in and out.
But you, a diplomat, a friend
wished me happy birthday, pushed your young grandson
through the zoo.

You knew you were going, heading toward this soaked hill.
You did all the teaching you could, boosting the young
to keep up the celebration.

After your service, from inside the car,
I saw how the rain ran in small rivers
down the windows.
It seemed the gravestones
shook and shimmered, stifled their laughter.

Nonsense
that you are not sitting here with us on damp chairs
tipping toward the Potomac.
It's now time to speak *of* you,
not to you, keeper of the family.
We can't help to notice
how sunlit skies pushed the rainstorm away.

Spending Time

In memory of departed classmates

I think of you and all my extra days
how spent. Now spent.
Sun sparkles on the bay.
A comet travels across the centuries.
There's a touch of very silken skin,
taste of Chardonnay.
I raise a glass!
Here's to all I never did this year.
Here's to all you never did again.
Driving that car, wind in your face,
a walk to the library on an autumn evening,
strolling arm and arm with your dad,
and then *he* was gone.
Did we view those Adirondack sunsets
as if they would last forever?

You and I shared a birthday.
Your boyhood home was down the road
from my middle age workplace.
We lived in the same large city,
but our paths never crossed.
Our journeys wound round the world.
The children grew, we recorded our lives
or left too quickly, leaving a smile
and a black band of remembrance across a page.

You and I talked at our last reunion,
not imagining it would be your last.
You gave me advice and said,
"I think *that's* most amazing to me.

The varied and fascinating lives
our classmates have lived."
And now you have moved on from
where it started for all of us, here,
snow chalking the mountains,
as we go down, wood smoke in the air.
the creek, swollen by the side of the road.

Boulanger's "D'un Vieux Jardin (of an old garden)"

We hear a friend play the piano
against a windowed gray sky.
We look at the branches of large trees
holding the solid gray in their limbs.
We crane our necks to see a
pattern against the bleakness.

Can you hear the green gardens of Rome,
endless sun and fountains splashing with water?
The notes rise and rise, buoyed by dancing measures
and large green leaves.
Then, just unable to stay afloat, the notes fall
past the garden's marble cherubim, pot-marked by the years,

The girl, Boulanger, would die four years after writing the music.
She, dead against branches cutting a solid gray sky into pieces.
My friend plays her notes that hold the hope of laughing water,
children running circular paths in the garden.
The music vaults higher and higher,
before cascading with the rainwater
that has bathed this land all spring.

Our misting faces turn upwards,
then down to the piano keys.
Each note rises to the branches,
holding the sky for sun.

Emily Dickinson

closed doors,
slammed them,
turned the lock.
She kept inside,
as she opened words
like doors,
sliced them open,
like tin cans
splashing out pain of a meadow
aching with dandelions.

Words in slanted scrawl
like skeins of wool
hidden in shut desk drawers,
scratched out on scraps,
on gilded stationery.

Emily Dickinson died
after crafting
an eternity of deaths,
syllables whirling
in eddies
like needles poking through
her unlived centuries.

I search for that phrase
pulled back through the eye
to a green, grassy space,
a candle in a midnight room.

On Viewing Childe Hassam

We all looked at the beautiful pictures
painted in a time before we were born,
in a century before the last one,
before the horrors of just yesterday
and the day before.
And we drank in the colors of the roses
whose petals had fallen on the table.

A woman looked into a mirror beside an open window.
The sunlight poured into the room filled with daffodils.
It was morning, and a younger woman was reading on a settee.
She was wearing a dress and stockings.
Why not?
It was a beautiful world, this world of the painting.
It was the world that preceded our childhoods or the childhoods we never had.

In the painting where the sun didn't shine,
there was the shimmering of wet city pavement.
Mothers took children by the hand
and led them to a warm and comfortable place.
The city had a clear view of blue sky
down to the harbor.

In the world of the heart, when a grassy lawn leads up to a clapboard house,
it means the ocean is a stone's throw away.

Lunch is almost ready, and the aroma of lilies and lilacs
overwhelms the senses
We don't need to strain the ear to make out the music.

A woman in lace plays the piano, while her sister sits nearby.
Softly, close the door so as not to disturb the slow cadence
of the passing years.

Artist's Studio

The artist swipes the salmon stone
with a wet cloth,
shakes his head at me.
"We go way back," he said.

The man I knew as a child
cuts and shapes pink marble,
white marble, pink and gray.

Pieces large enough to embrace,
carried here from the same swath
Michelangelo saw in Carrara
as his Mary, her Son,
and David.

Today, in this New England garden,
the river rises when it rains,
but doesn't flood the stone, the studio.

On the street, as I quit the space
I'll never see again,
curled leaves scrape
along the concrete sidewalk,
dust moves under dark, dry clouds.

Will the marble change to soft marsh,
water rising over the fish market, the boatyard,
desert sweeping west?

In the green town where you and I grew up
my parents lie, side by side.

Sometimes, I wipe their stones clean,
break up the hard-packed earth,
as we wait for the rain to sculpt
a dry memory.

Photograph on a Foggy Winter Afternoon

How the sun comes in from the left, in shafts.
How it sits on the leaves that have wintered on that tree.
How it lights up the mist to white,
sparing the dark forest floor.

How we know this is an interlude
between ice and ice,
that the ghost will return,
sharpening and sharpening into focus
on the summer hillside.

They say, our dead appear in photographs.
How have I never seen?
How her lips smile and part,
How the moon turns murky
above the inland marsh.
How this scene in the woods
is already gone, stuck in the album pages,
lifted up through the mist
on a warm, winter day.

Deer

I looked for them again
but there was only
dappled summer sunshine
where a mother deer and her fawn
had stepped out of the trees
the day before.

They crossed in front of me,
sauntered across a lawn and
entered the woods
alongside someone's backyard.

It had happened.
And yes it was a gift
as true as
visits from super-naturals
and orbs and faces
that come up behind the eyelids
smiling.

As true as dreams of a car
crashing into a childhood dining room
and a car smashing into
a deer that crosses a winter road.

With the sound of hide to tin,
it somersaults into a glade,
and makes its final pinwheel resting place.

They say that impact
doesn't mean death,

but shock to the nerves.
And I saw the body, as if in sleep.

Does a child know where those places are?
Where deer can safely cross a road?
Where forgiving paints the meadow?

A fawn walks with his mother
in summer sunlight
and they walk at night, in a mountain forest
before sleep takes us all.

3. A World of Sunrise

These Four o'Clock Days

How did it become four o'clock gray?
Skylight turning dark,
houses fastening
their tuxedo fronts.

Just two months ago we
shuttered the neighborhood pool,
toasting with canned margaritas.
Four weeks ago, we waited for a full,
shredded moon to rise above the Danube.

My five-year-old granddaughter adjusts
to the fact of darkness,
how there is no longer the beach,
wrapped in a towel,
sun nodding past Manomet Point.

I've heard that in Hungary, people are never
prepared for the first snowfall, and so
the streets remain unplowed.

Here on the eastern-most part of North America,
the light leaves earlier and earlier each day.
Sudden twilight.
How could it happen?
Five hours slip away and hide in a beach dune,
as a gull turns a nonchalant eye
toward a crumpled coffee cup filled with sand.

Window Witch

A witch's head floats in the window
of a local coffee shop two days
after All Hallows' Eve.
Small pointed hat,
straight straw hair.
a silhouette,
black against the sea-white
of a seaside street.

When she could, she used her broom
to flick off dust from old books,
from witches' tales.
No saint, she, the day the graveyards empty.
Spirits rise in straight lines, arms by their sides.
like Irish step dancers.

Her spirit sails up the cold coast
to the town where the witch hangings were,
flesh and bone,
pilloried on the words of children.
They say hysteria? Moldy bread?
Neighborly disputes?

A witch visited my early nightmares
sitting in a corner chair in my grandparents' dark hallway.
Another rose from a small rock beside my bed.
to move to the window.

A silhouette frightening me out of sleep,
following me through Halloweens
to the coffee shop window.

A drumbeat rain on the glass,
a witch glued to the pane.
Never to be stored,
Only storied, visiting my dreams,

Wooster Square, 2020

It was early March that year
when I took a photo
from our rented living room in New Haven.
My photo shows patterns, a room spare in its simplicity.

The sky was blue, clear and absolute,
through a half-moon window.

The reflection of the sunlit window on the wall
was more real than the window itself.
And balancing above was a scalloped clock
showing 2:55 p.m.
If I had known, could I have stopped the hands,
pulled them down and counter to what was to come?

That apartment was nestled between two funeral homes,
caskets coming and going
in the parking lots.
We didn't know what was ahead.

Across the street, through the window, was a white house
with shadows cast by a large, leafless tree.
Had I read the signs,
I would have paid heed to a dream
I had that same week,
in the time before the sickness.

I had been sentenced to prison
for something I did.
The jail was a big, airy, sunny room lined with windows.
I had my clothes with me for the prison term,
and I hung them on coat racks.

When more people entered the room, I was surprised
that I wouldn't be alone.
I removed my clothes from the racks.
Then, a woman and I walked outside on a path surrounded
by tall, arching trees that made a domed covering.

I could leave the prison
to take walks during the time
that started before we knew it,
long before the sun made patterns
on the wall of a lost world.

Cape Cod Bay

There are unhappy spirits here . . .
Wives overboard, dead babies,
Indians caught in the claws of plague
and those too weak to bury them.

Heads on spikes, skulls in sand dunes,
death in the planting fields.

Have the spirits left the beaches,
the rough surf,
a million sun flecks on Cape Cod Bay?
Now come the tourists to Plymouth Rock,
to the Italianate tower at Provincetown,
white man's stones piled to mark the landing,

The Mayflower's women washed clothing
In freshwater ponds on their first trip off the ship.
How the water must have tasted to drink!
How the sun shone, teasing the visitors,
settling in to killing cold.

The wind still whispers through these inland pines . . .
wives overboard, dead babies,
Indians caught in the claws of plague.
We gape at a tooth hidden
beneath a single maple leaf.

Beach

There's always a slice of sunlight
on the ocean
at Kalmus Beach.
Whether in winter,
or late fall,
it mirrors a seagull
as a boat sails right through it.

The light seems to come from water's depth—
there's no sun above.
It divides gray from gray,
leaving equal parts of gloom.
on either side.

It points to joy on the shore,
hope for summer far out
beyond the cove,
the island.

It points to all our loves not realized,
unfocused and shimmering
on the ocean's surface,
always a horizon away.

Maine Sunrise

Light spreads
from a nugget of night
both ways over the water
at Little Sheepscot.

I step gingerly down those old wooden stairs
a few hours after June's midnight
and see a flaming sky over the gray river.

It's what I disbelieve in November,
when days are lopped off at either end,
absorbing black
like ink in a white cloth.

But here, in the old house, the mirror,
pot-marked and rusted,
catches the whole view of the river
from the wall across the room.
A reflection of these summer days
that are long enough to hold a small boat heading up
the middle of the watercourse in the morning
and back again, wake gleaming, in
waning light of a long evening.

From the damp woods, filled with trees
upright and fallen during the winter,
I can hear a boat heading around the point,
voices climbing over the motor's raucous growl.

All is stilled when deep darkness falls
for a few hours, and light once more
presses against cloth curtains
at the upstairs window.

Marigot

The waiter took our order
beside the darkened, quiet water.
A father, mother and son speaking French
steered their small boat
into a slip.
The quiet soaked up what had been laughter,
white lights strung out along the marina.
Now, the quiet still held
the hurricane that had raked across the island
of the sunrise, coral, turquoise sea.
The marina had rocked with good food, good cheer.

Now, restaurants are boarded up, docks gone, life sucked out.
Dark energy fills empty spaces
once filled by the winds that blew this place down.
Close your eyes and see the wind,
sand rising in sheets, water
rising, higher and higher.
See buildings flat, roofs peeling back like tin cans.
The sun is nowhere.
It's been wiped out.
How deep are the clouds, how high is the ocean?
If we stand on our heads, will it be like it was?

A bright orange shawl flies
over the town from the flea market.
You can hear our daughters laughing, sitting atop ponies
that carry them through the forest.

The boy and his parents weren't laughing now,
on a vacation in a dark land,
They steered their small boat
away from this marina
to another harbor.

Caribbean Rising

The first time I heard the sun rise,
it woke me from sleep in Guadeloupe.
It was a sound like a wind blowing,
and the birds were caught up in it,
and the sky brightened to white light.

In Simpson Bay, I watched as
the sun toiled up behind the hills,
and the trade winds
blew in from the east,
nudging the goldenness.

The doves woke,
and the fireball lit up
the back of the cloudbank to bright pink
that drained away
to a white-heated day.

Northward, the sun rises over the Potomac
as the river widens into the sea
off the Maryland shore.

Sun with the sound of
all our days,
the wake of the fisherman's boat
catches its early light.
Its dusky pink
lightens the river
taking a prism path to that southern sea
where I first heard the sunrise,
brightening the sky to white light
waking the doves beyond the cloudbank.

Dominoes

You can let color into your life if you want to.
For years, we watched a black and white television
propped up at the end of our bed.
Dancers moved in colorless patterns,
gray Jack O'lanterns sparking white flames.

In the landscape today out this window,
black clouds are lightening down to bright white
just above the tree line.
The trees are bare, feathery black;
Gray shingles lie below a white strip of flat roof.

The scream of the black crow enters my Technicolor dream
where keening from a woman's throat
hurls me out of sleep
toward a bird high on a dead tree branch.
At this hour, the sky turns gray
and then white.

Soon, the sun will rise,
but don't look directly at it.
Instead, remember the neon reds flashing against a deep salmon sunset,
the blue of the harbor at the edge of the world,
the green of the meadow just before the light, and you, left.

Monument Valley

Sun rising over Connecticut woods,
Minnesota lakes,
Colorado mountains
and Monument Valley mesas.

It reddens blocks of petrified strata,
pushed and folded,
a thousand feet high.

My life measured against them
is like a hummingbird's heartbeat
fluttering against the mountains.

Valley that was in turn river, swamp and desert,
home to nomads crouching in the stones' shadows,
antelopes etched on the sandstone slabs.

How to measure good and evil against these rocks?
How to measure time?
See the rocks as earth's sculptures,
testaments to the rising and setting of the ancient sun.

See them as towering backdrops to the
Navaho hogans clustered near the caves,
to campfires, and the wispy smoke that spirits away
before it reaches the boulders' knees.

How to pray for us, here?
Who would hear, but the wind and the sunlight
that travels up the rockface and over the valley
cratered with the bones of the buffalo.

Tucson

I sit
on a shining
hardwood floor
and look out
at a 6 a.m. gray sky.
All night, the wind whips
in and out of the room.
A train whistle cries
across the desert.
And because it's unknown land,
it could be a train
going from nowhere
to nowhere.

Lonely is a house
sitting on a patch
of southwest sand.
Lonely is a sunset of red,
pink and gold
with a strip of blue.

Seville Sunday

The call of the dove fills space
between church bell chime and trellis
climbing up the walls of our tiny patio.
Only a square of sky blue sends down the hottest air.

In triple coo, the bird asks,
"Where have you gone?
Where are you going?
Where are you?"

In more frantic tremolo, its call echoes down the years, the
    centuries
through the gardens of the Alcazar and the warm fountains,
making a beeline to the Azores and across the ocean in mist, time-
    traveler.
It resounds in my grandmother's dining room.
"Listen!" she said to me.
"It's the mourning dove."

It was the owl hooting in the woods
to the little girl lost and far from home.

Or that Eurasian dove call
moving across the snow tops east of the Alhambra
to fall on the cupped ears
thirsty and far below.

Massachusetts

Forsythia was blooming
on the cold April day
my grandson was baptized in Plymouth
in an old stone church.

Babies were baptized in the forest here in 1620,
and later inside the meetinghouse.
There was violence fermented by loose talk, threats,
violence of illness, typhus.

The Pilgrims walked inland 40 miles
on empty stomachs to keep peace,
to make peace.
It is said they cured the sachem Massasoit
with fruit preserves.

Along with corn,
the sachem planted seeds of thought . . .
trading land for beads and coats,
gaining hatchets and moose-skins for fish-full rivers,
red-hued trees, skull-sacked dunes
and summer-heated fields.

The Pilgrims survived on a rare full meal,
shrunken, fevered prayers,
as newborn babies, breached westward,
peppered the spirit-filled coast.

Some Pilgrims stayed to die,
drawn by the pull of the sea.
They watched the harbor for a ship,
sweeping pottery out a kitchen door.

They watch from the cemetery above the town,
blue water stained with white sails.
Young river herring move from the sea
up the same ancient stream
the Pilgrims glimpsed from the ship.
They wonder why they didn't walk westward from
that rocky street sprouting up from the bay;
Why they didn't turn their backs
slung with their babies,
and take an inland trail toward the sunset.

What We Have, in Plymouth

I look down at Plymouth Rock,
that may or may not be.
The rock was dragged, hoisted, dropped, broken. chipped.
It deserves to be the rock, the anchor,
washed over and over by the tides,
the water leaves ripples of sand that frame the rock,
a wet shade of its former self.

It was saved, they say,
by a 94-year-old man whose father told him
in 1791 that it was the rock the Pilgrims met in the harbor
at the end of their journey.

Tiger Lily was tied to Skull Rock as the tide rose
up to her chin. She was saved by Peter Pan.
Wild monkeys scamper over that stone in Gibraltar
where two seas meet.
Myth has it that Scottish giant Benandonner
walked over the slippery, smooth rocks of the Giants' Causeway
to cross the Irish sea, up to no good.

The *story* of Plymouth Rock is more real than the rock itself.
Housed in its grand pavilion at the edge of the harbor,
we learn from it about hardship and brokenness,
about strength and survival.

On cold, cloudy winter days,
we look back past Cole's Hill.
See the rock's columns just coming into view
and the masts of the Mayflower down the coast?
What a story they tell!

It's carried by gulls
across more seas,
nuggets of truth caught in their beaks.

Boston

Today, I walk up Beacon Hill
from the hospital side.
The catching of the breath, the slow trudge
are new.
50 years ago, I climbed the hill from the other side,
walking up Mt. Vernon Street to my new job.
College degree, resume, and pay phone calls
to my soon-to-be boss, who tired
and hired me.

I suppose the dogwood bloomed those long-ago springs
as they bloom this year.
Daffodils spilled out over low metal fences.
Car tires, like popping bubblegum,
Drove over the cobblestones.

I was careless to look, in those days,
trekking through the Public Garden
in Dr. Scholl's sandals.
Careless to look at those spring blossoms.
Careless not to hide secrets.
Careless to leave the city it would take 50 years to visit again.

Today, we never found my old street,
but I didn't have to revisit the place
to know that our young voices echoed
over the bricks on the way to the Boston Common
where Kathy found her little boy lost
amidst Hari Krishna mantras.

I didn't know there would be hills to climb
before I found this one again.
As I reach its summit,
I ask,
Do you remember me?
The girl beginning her slow climb
without a care?

About the Author

Susan Hunter has been writing poetry all her adult life as she pursued careers in the book publishing and newspaper fields and raised three daughters. She was a newspaper editor in Connecticut and is currently a freelance reporter for newspapers in Massachusetts.

Her chapbook, *Unfinished Spaces*, was recently published by Finishing Line Press. She's had poetry published in *On the Seawall, One Page Poetry Anthology, American Literary Review, Southern Humanities Review, Saranac Journal, The Chaffin Journal, Poem* and *Illya's Honey*.

She was a general contributor at the Bread Loaf Writers Conference in 2018. Her verse has been featured on Cape and Islands NPR radio and on local television arts shows in Plymouth, MA.

The themes of her poems focus on her family, on loss, and in a more positive view, on transition.

Raised in Princeton, NJ, she received a BA in English from Middlebury College and an MA in English literature from New York University.

She and her husband live in Plymouth, MA.

www.ingramcontent.com/pod-product-compliance
Lightning Source LLC
Chambersburg PA
CBHW070936160426
43193CB00011B/1710